The Art of iPhone Review

Why the iphone can't be beat (Higher Education Edition)

Preface:

Subjective review within a reasonable framework.

Notice:

This book is for professionals, as it assumes that you have some prior knowledge and experience of industrial design. Most of the parts will not contain any step-by-step instructions, detailed explanations, or practical examples, as they will focus on the advanced aspects and applications of the subject.

A lot of times, people don't know what they want even if you show it to them until someone tells them.

Because of the size of the mobile phone, every detail will be zoomed in. So we need a whole framework to get a comprehensive review, so here is this logical book. In order to recognize the logic layers, I will add the Roman number before the items to show their grade.

I The next generation of mobile phones in my imagination

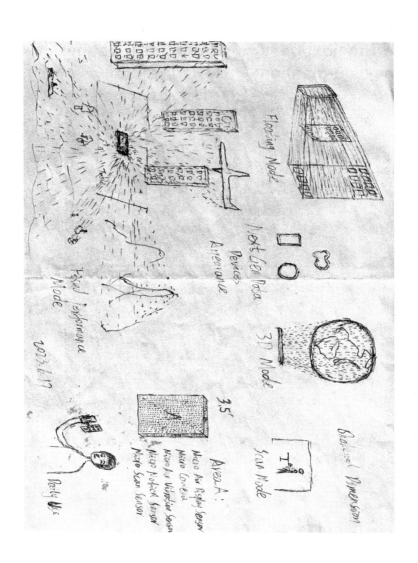

1. Looking the screen area that pupils focus on.
2. The default finger operation area is the above area

1. Looking the EOG's space area.
2. Vibrate the air in the above area to make sounds.

Bend your palm to adjust the distance between the display area and the data device.

Move your palm upward to change to 3D mode.
Move your palm downward to change to 2D mode.

Lock

Sensor blocked solution
Ensure that 70% of the sensors can support full device operation.
When some of the sensors are blocked, Reinitialize the entire work to the remaining normal sensors.

Palm Hold + Rotation
Resize the display area.
2023. 6.17
Shortened Dimension

5

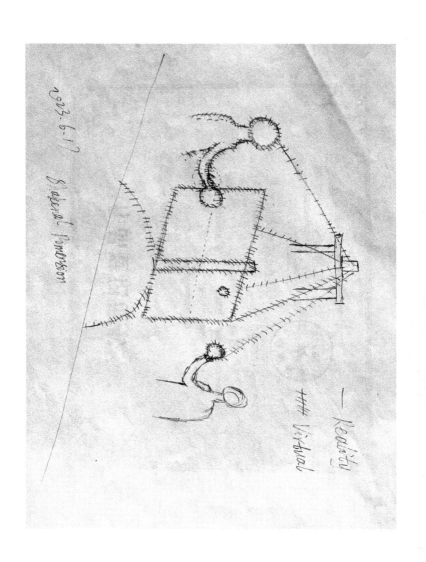

2023-6-17

Slabenal Submisson

— Reality
Virtual

/ Special Tips

1. The ultimate aim of developing the digital world is to simulate and enhance the real world, while the ultimate aim of developing the real world is to integrate and benefit from the digital world. However, they can never fully achieve or replace each other, and they can only coexist and evolve together.

2. User experience is how users feel and think when they interact, use, and recall the product or service that meets their needs. The product or service can be hardware- or software-based. User experience depends on both the physical senses - touch, hearing, smell, taste, and sight - and the mental senses - efficiency, interference, completion, and emotion - when satisfying the instincts of survival, reproduction, passing time.

3. The items of equal level are listed in order of importance. In perspective, the ratio of up items /down items is above 1.2, but the result depends on the actual situation.

4. For any item, the minimum acceptable score is 6 out of 10. No items with lower scores needed to be evaluated. Items with higher scores have a superior

level of industrial design that requires more advanced review.

5. The more important an area is or the longer the eye lingers on, the more sensitive the senses react to it.
6. Any item should avoid two parallel concepts, styles, or elements at the same time.
7. If one of the sub-items of an item makes up more than 96% of it, the other sub-item with a smaller proportion will look more abrupt.
8. There are two types of brain consumption modes: low brain consumption and high brain consumption. Low brain consumption modes are easy to remember and use less brain resources. Examples are muscle memory and conditioned reflexes. High brain consumption modes are hard to remember and use more brain resources. Examples are handling information, analyze, and judging. These are two concepts that are clear in theory but vague in practice. The basic and bottom logical operations should follow the principle of low brain consumption mode. That is why we should avoid double-side-interacting (on a mobile phone with normal size).
9. Compartmentalization is a concept that perceives things differently. It affects how people react to things. For mobile phones, we can use different senses to classify compartmentalization. For example, visual,

auditory, tactile, psychological, single, and comprehensive. For instance, the interface of the lock screen and the home screen in unlocked mode are different visual compartments. The home screen, the left screen of the home screen, and the App library are also different visual compartments on the same level. The top swipe, bottom swipe, left swipe, and right swipe on the home screen are different interactive compartments on the same level. Single-finger click, single-finger swipe, and single-finger long press are different interactive compartments on the same level. There are two rules for compartmentalization: 1) The fewer sub-items, the more interactive precision and efficiency. 2) To keep the low brain consumption mode, the interactive methods of the same layer should be fewer than four.

10. You can delete some items based on the actual review situations when necessary.

11. This is a theoretical idea. To get closer to the Tao, you need to study harder and harder about the ecosystem of mobile phones. What is Tao? Let's look at the original iPhone's 3.5" screen, which is a manifestation of the Tao. 3.5" that is the result of balancing the hand sizes of potential users from different countries and ages. It is a concept of love, to make the product fit the user's comfort as much as possible. This is how a

product should be. But now the increasing screen size makes more users tolerate its poor grip experience, which is far from the Tao.

12. Any component that does not work as expected throughout the life cycle of the product - except for special designs that allow consumers to replace the consumable components by themselves - needs to rely on professional repair solutions to fix the problem. This is a design flaw that shows a serious quality issue. For example, sacrifice the battery's life cycle for fast charging.

13. The world of design has three levels. The first level is the countries of old money and pleasure-seeking, like Britain and France. The second level is efficient and modernistic countries, like the United States. The third level is conservative countries, like Japan.

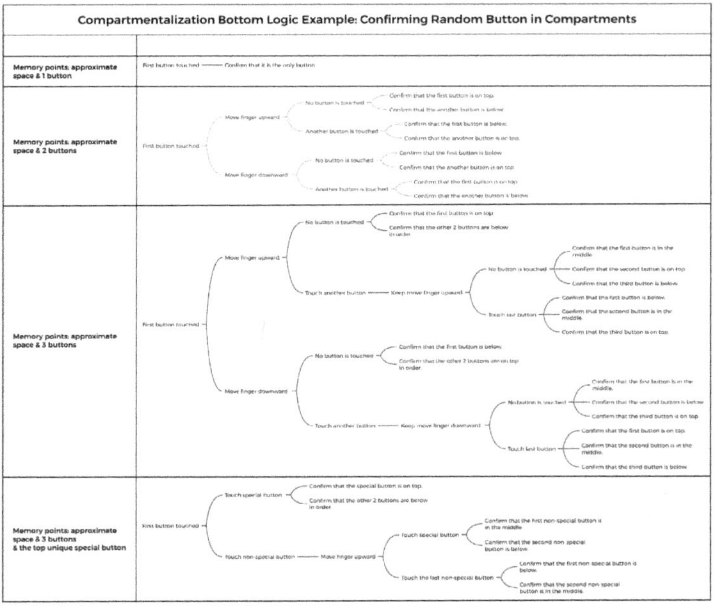

/ Design concept

There are two types of mobile phone design concept: conventional and non-conventional. The conventional part of a non-conventional mobile phone must score at least 6 out of 10 to pass, and its non-conventional part must score around 8 out of 10 to be excellent.

II Conventional design concept (otherwise it is non-conventional)

III Balance: It is based on Tao, which means keeping the backward parts in the most balanced position as possible. For example, the smaller fonts get a more exquisite look, but they are hard to read if they are too small.

III Humanity: Tools were made to serve human needs, not to make humans suffer their flaws. For example, people enjoy the colorful world in daylight, so don't tell me that OLED's dark mode saves power and OLED avoids the power-saving problems of the light mode. This is what technology should improve, not what marketing misleads users to change their natural lifestyle.

III Entire unity: This means following the same design concepts for every component and every design element.

III Exquisite (elegant): This means pursuing the highest visual information per inch and the perfect combination of visual information.

III Extreme: This means pursuing perfection in every detail.

III Efficiency: This means that it is simple, clear, and natural. No confusion, no detour.

III Best visual-efficiency: This means providing a better visual design for the same functional purpose.

II The entire implementation of the design concept

III Level of functional requirements and user experience

III Level of psychological & emotional resonance

III Level of sight

IV Level of hardware & software

V Level of hardware

1. Level of sight (Surface: inside = 7:3)
2. Level of touch
3. Level of hearing
4. Level of product quality: raw material, quality, safety, craft

V Level of software

1. Level of OS
2. Level of app
3. Level of page
4. Level of the message: graphics, texts, shapes, objects, etc.

5. Level of basic elements of sight: points, lines, surfaces, colors, space, etc.

III Level of personal & others' actual perception

III The best example of the entire implementation

Apple has an entire uniform and exquisite concept of using the curve of God in everything. The curve of God is the curvature of the rounded corners that you can see in many details. For example, on the iPhone, you can see the curve of God in the metal frame, the physical buttons, the rear bump, the camera, the notch / Dynamic Island, the screen, the Lighting connector, and even some internal components on printed circuit board.

In the software, you can see the curve of God in the app icons, the dock, the search bar, the settings bar, the control center, the notification bar in the notification center, the widget, and the notch / Dynamic Island.

The curve of God is also present in other products, such as the MacBook and its software. And even in Apple's buildings and facilities, such as the Apple Park visitor center, trash cans, and seats.

The curve of God is a legacy of Mr. Jobs - who made sure that everything Apple did had a high level of entire unity and elegance across hardware, software, product, and company.

III A common bad example of the entire implementation

This simple page has different types of visual and interactive elements.

The title section has no visual interaction but has input interaction. The date section has a half-screen pop-up visual interaction and click interaction. The time section has input and click interactions. The location section has a full-screen pop-up visual interaction and input interaction.

The repeat section has a bottom visual interaction and a click interaction.

The interactions within each section are not uniform, coherent, or intuitive. They are fragmented and reduce efficiency. The details matter a lot. To make this beautiful page even better, we should try to reduce the non-uniform and non-natural interactions.

/ Entire design style/language

There are two types of mobile phone design style/ language: conventional and non-conventional. The conventional part of a non-conventional mobile phone must score at least 6 out of 10 to pass, and its non-conventional part must score around 8 out of 10 to be excellent.

II Conventional design style (otherwise it is non-conventional)

III Big popular

1. Minimalist
2. Classical or Retro

III Popular

1. Art
2. Luxurious

II Principles of design element: The finishing touch without breaking the premise of the entire design concept and design style.

II Design concepts cover everywhere. Design styles/languages mainly cover surfaces.

/ Chapter 1 Comprehensive optimization of hardware and software

Excellent products have a balance between software and hardware, and between design and function. The ratio of software strength to hardware strength should be from 6:4 to 4.5:5.5, gradually inferior, and the ratio of design to function should be from 6:4 to 4:6, gradually inferior.

II Industrial design of hardware

III Sight

IV Entire sight

1. The distance affects how you see something for the
    first time. Usually, you should choose 1/2 meters within

your own view and 2 meters outside other people's view to evaluate the first impression. You should make sure that the product looks perfect from both distances and both views.

2. The best principles of visual unity: the design elements have a continuous and united appearance without any breaks or interruptions. This applies to color, shape, and structure.

3. The best principles of visual coordination: the design elements follow some proportions that are pleasing and natural to the human. For example, symmetry and golden ratio. A small amount of non-conventional design on top of this can make the product more interesting and attractive in a short time.

4. The best principles of color: first, you should think about how color affects the psychology of the user. Then, you should think about the role of color in the product. Finally, you should think about the color itself. According to the theory of static and dynamic, the used colors, like the static world, the new colors, like the dynamic elements, the new colors will instantly become the focus, while the used colors will not attract too much attention. For product design, you should aim for a continuous and uniform appearance of the design elements, or avoid any interruptions or breaks. This includes the colors of the front panel, frame, and

rear panel. For color itself, it is divided into different levels of colors based on the times that humans see. The color of the highest level is the color of the air, which is the most seen color by humans, but humans cannot make it. The closest thing to air is glass, which can create a 3D color effect by superimposing on other colors. This is a miracle that breaks the common sense that the eye can only see 2D colors in the natural world. The color of the second-best level is the color of the sky, which is the second most seen color by humans, especially during the day. The color of the third-best level is the color of the human body, which is the most familiar color to humans, such as the colors of skin and hair. The color of the fourth-best level is the color of nature, which is the second most familiar color to humans. The color of the fifth-best level is the artificial color. Monochrome is the cornerstone, and the color combination - the same color system can reduce the sense of abruptness, the near color secondarily - the esthetics of gradient are stricter, and the premise is that made the best product of monochrome - no more expand needed here. The more the design concept focuses on minimalism, the more it favors monochrome.

5. The best principles of line and shape: straight lines are the basic and simple form, while curves are more

complex and beautiful. Curves can be inward or outward, depending on how they can be bent. Inward curves are more aggressive, while outward curves are more expansive. Outward curves are easier to handle than inward curves. The curve belongs to God, and is a kind of orderly cognition distilled from chaos. Order meets order will improve each other, but order meets disorder will return to the basics of chaos or be weakened. Visuals of a physical pure curve with a psychological straight line are the best, a curve-based straight line is the second best, a straight-based curve line is the third best, and a pure straight line is the fourth best. This is because a straight line feels more harmful than a curve in a product. For example, the iPhone 14 Pro's flatted frame is more uncomfortable to grip than the iPhone 11 Pro's rounded frame. The shape of the design elements and electronic components should be consistent with or close to the shape of the body, i.e. quadrilateral, and the number of edges of multiple shapes should not be more or less.

6. The best principles of material gloss: a non-mirror-like material looks all the same in any environment, but a mirror-like material changes with the light and the surroundings. The same material can have different visual effects by using different crafts and different grades. But it is hard to change the quality of the

material by using the same craft on different grades of the same material. Some materials have a charm that is not only based on their features, but also on how they interact with the environment. For example, precious metals can reflect light and show a unique visual effect, even if they are very similar to other elements. The best visual effect is when some of the light is reflected and some of it stands out in the gloss of the material. The second best is when there is no reflection at all. The third best is when there is a mirror-like reflection - it creates complex scenes that are hard to control.

7. The best principles of thickness: the thinner the mobile phone, the better the technical integration and the better visual effect. It also makes the mobile phone get a better grip experience.

IV Sight of front

1. The best principles of touchscreen integration: the whole screen is better than the non-whole screen, and the screen with an internal independent non-whole part is better than the screen with a non-whole part

bordered with the bezel. And the treatment of the non-whole part should greatly reduce the sense of existence.

2. The best principles of screen-to-body ratio: the higher the screen-to-body ratio, the more impressive the visual effect. The curved screen expands the screen-to-body ratio, which is more impressive when compared to a flatted screen.

3. The best principles of the uniform width of edge bezels : the larger the inconsistency of the visual area, the worse the visual effect, the larger the inconsistent difference in width of edge bezels, the worse the visual effect.

4. The best principles of uniform four edge bezels: four edge bezels with equal width are best. The larger difference of the edge bezel width between the maximum and the minimum, the worse the visual effect; the larger difference of the edge bezel width between the adjacent bezels, the worse the visual effect.

5. The less area of the effective content display that is affected by the non-whole part, the better. In just two years, the bottom of the iPhone 13's notch and iPhone 14 Pro's Dynamic Island have been moved down

twice. This has made the area of effective content display decrease at least 4% forever.

IV Sight of rear

1. The best principles of uniform rear panel: Minimalist is the best design choice for rear panel. If there are some design compromises due to industrial limitations, they should be minimized as much as possible.
2. The best principles of uniform color: the color of the highest level is the color of the air, which is the most seen color by humans, but humans cannot make it. The closest thing to air is glass, which can create a 3D color effect by superimposing on other colors. This is a miracle that breaks the common sense that the eye can only see 2D colors in the natural world. The color of the second-best level is the color of the sky, which is the second most seen color by humans, especially during the day. The color of the third-best level is the color of the human body, which is the most familiar color to humans, such as the colors of skin and hair. The color of the fourth-best level is the color of nature, which is the second most familiar color to humans. The color of the fifth-best level is the artificial color.

Monochrome is the cornerstone, and the color combination - the same color system can reduce the sense of abruptness, the near color secondarily - the esthetics of gradient are stricter, and the premise is that made the best product of monochrome - no more expand needed here. The more the design concept focuses on minimalism, the more it favors monochrome.

3. The best principles of uniform shape: The best shape is a two-dimensional plane, which means there is no bump or protrusion on the surface. If there is a bump, it looks worse. The bigger and higher the bump, the worse it looks. The shape of the design elements and electronic components should be consistent with or close to the shape of the body, i.e. quadrilateral, and the number of edges of multiple shapes should not be more or less.

4. The best principles of uniform physical structure: The best structure is a no-cut rear panel, which means there is no gap or slit on the rear panel. If there is a cut, it should be very small and not noticeable.

IV Sight of side

1. The best principles of uniform of the four sides: the four sides of the mobile phone should look the same, in terms of color and shape. The best consistency is when the four sides have the same color and shape, which makes the product look uniform.

2. The best principles of uniform physical structure: the product should not have any cuts or gaps on its surface. The best structure is when the product is whole and seamless, which makes it look smooth and flawless. If there are any cuts or gaps, they should be small and not noticeable.

3. The best principles of physical buttons and holes: port-less is the best. The second-best design of button and hole is when they follow some proportions - symmetry, golden ratio, and regular ratio - that are pleasing to the eyes.

4. The best principles of the curved screen / waterfall display: the left and right sides are part of the front sight.

II Touch

III Static Touch

1. The best touching experience is like touching the baby's skin. The second-best experience is like touching the skin. The third best touch experience is smoothest with minimum friction.
2. The best principles of precise and smooth: a touching experience that should not feel rough or sharp. The more precise and smoother the touch, the better.
3. The best principles of sense of damping and vein: this depends on the individual.
4. The best principles of softness: the softer the touch, the better the user experience. The best feeling is like touching the baby's skin - followed by skin.
5. The best principles of the grip experience: touch that should fit well with your palm for more comfort. The larger the contact area between your palm and the mobile phone, the more secure you will feel.
6. The best principles of control: the smaller the size of the mobile phone, the easier it is to control with your palm and the better the experience. However, the size should still be within the range of control.

7. The best principles of fixation: determined by the inclusiveness of the palm, the mobile phone should match the size and shape of your palm. The shape of the mobile phone should be convenient for one-hand holding. Generally, spherical and oval shapes are better than rectangular and square shapes.

8. The best principles of pressure: consider the pressure of the hand and center of gravity, you should focus on the hand's feels instead of the weight of mobile phone. The center of gravity of the mobile phone should be in the middle or lower part of your palm when you hold it. This will make it more stable and comfortable. For example, if you hold a mobile phone that is too heavy at the top, it will feel unstable and uncomfortable.

9. The best principles of temperature: the temperature should not be too hot or too cold while holding the mobile phone. The best temperature is the same as the ambient temperature, unless there is something unusual. This is because people are used to the ambient temperature and do not feel any discomfort. If the temperature is hotter or colder than the ambient temperature, it may affect the grip experience.

10. The best principles of humidity: the humidity should match the humidity of the environment. The solid and gaseous forms are better for low humidity. The grip experience will not change too much if the humidity is

within a comfortable range. However, if the humidity is too high or too low, it may affect the grip experience.

11. The best principles of hardness: It should have a suitable hardness for your grip experience. The higher the hardness, the better quality you may feel.

12. The best principles of sense of intrusion: the more sticky, rough, or sharp the touch, the more intrusive you feel and the worse the experience.

III Dynamic

IV Slide on screen

The best slide experience is sliding with low damping. The lower the damping, the easier it is to move your finger on the screen and the better the user experience.

IV Vibration

1. The best principles of restoration of real physical touch: the closer to reality, the better.

2. The best principles of response speed: the faster the touch response, the better.

3. The best principles of the non-linear strength curve: the perfect vibration, is that from a faster change of gradually increased strength to a slower change of gradually decreased strength smoothly. The smoother the curve changes, the more comfortable it feels. This is an advanced review item.

4. The best principles of frequency and amplitude: the closer to reality, the better, we should avoid being too extreme.

5. The best principles of duration: vibrating time should last as long as reality and avoid being too long or too short. The time of gradually increasing strength is shorter than the time of gradually decreasing strength. For example, a touch that lasts too long or too short makes you feel unnatural or uncomfortable.

II Hearing

III The resolution of real sound

The best principles: lossless music support is better than lossy music support.

IV DAC and op-amp chips

The best principles: Hifi is a starting point to appreciate music.

IV 3.5mm headphone jack

The best principles: the wired hearing experience is better than the wireless hearing experience.

IV Bluetooth

The best principles: A better way to rank the hearing
experience of different codecs is: LDAC > Apt-X > AAC.
This is only for listening, not for appreciating.

IV Sound performance

The sound quality depends on how well the codec can
reproduce different recorded environments. However,
different people may hear different sounds.

1. The best principles of pitch: performance is better
   when the codec can reproduce different recorded
   environments more accurately.
2. The best principles of loudness: performance is better
   when the codec can reproduce different recorded
   environments more accurately.
3. The best principles of color of tone: ① audio frequency
   (principle: The codec can cover the audio frequency
   that humans can hear, which is from 20 Hz to 20,000
   Hz. ②Response time (principle: the shorter, the better,
   excellent threshold is 10ms.) ③The spatial effect (The
   best codec is the one that can create a realistic sound

effect without distorted or lost any specific frequencies. It should also have a balanced ratio of sound quality and compression.)

4. The best principles of spatial sense: the codec should be able to reproduce the sound as if it is coming from a different shape, size, position, direction, and movement in the recorded environment.

5. The best principles of tuning style: the codec should be able to capture the details of the sound, such as the resolution, the atmosphere, the balance and connection of the three frequencies - low-frequency sound waves, middle-frequency sound waves, high-frequency sound waves, and the vocals and instruments. The codec also should be able to match the original recorded environments as close as possible. If the codec has a different tuning style from the original recorded environments, if it is not even bad, it should still be clear and pleasant. If the codec has a better tuning style than the original recorded environments, it is even better.

II Built quality

III Performance

IV Electronic Components - They are important, but not the highest factor to review.

The best principles: the main components of a flagship mobile phone should be high-end, while other components can be mid-range, but no more than 30% of them. The mobile phone should not use low-end components that would affect its performance in some situations, especially those related to the core calculation and transportation. Different companies have different abilities to negotiate with the suppliers, so the price never reflects the quality of the components.

I'm not a specifications fan. The specifications of an electronic component were not meant to reflect its grade and have nothing to do with the user experience. Every single specification can not reflect the comprehensive strength of the component. It is something only all specifications can do.

V Raw material grade

The best principles: this refers to the quality and purity of the materials that were used to make the components. The higher the raw material grade, the better the entire quality of the component.

V Craft technology

The best principles: this was how the component was made. More advanced craft technologies mean higher quality and a better guaranteed user experience. Higher power efficiency means longer battery life and less energy waste.

V Performance specifications

The best principles: the information should be showed detailed and accurate.

V The actual performance

The best principles: the closer the actual performance is to the theoretical performance, the better.

V Screen - the ultimate goal is to infinitely reproduce the visual effects that are close to the real world, to fake reality.

1. The best principles of color accuracy: it determines how close the colors of the screen are to the colors of the real world. The better the color accuracy, the more realistic the screen looks. The colors of the screen can be affected by different conditions, such as the color gamut, brightness, or the viewing angle of the screen. The smaller the $\triangle$E, the less difference there is between the colors of the screen and the colors of standard. The colors of the screen are formed by pixel dots, which are very small. If there is any difference between the pixel dots, it can form a bad screen. To avoid this situation, the pixel dots should be as consistent as possible. And the closer to 100% unification, bad pixels look more abruption.
2. The best principles of PPI - pixels per inch: logical PPI= $\sqrt{(\text{length pixels}^2+\text{width pixels}^2)}$/screen size. The more PPI the screen has, the clearer the screen looks, and the more realistic the visual information is.
3. The best principles of color gamut coverage: the bigger the color gamut, the more colors of the screen

can display. The color gamut is measured by how much of a standard color space it can cover. The current standard is DCI-P3, which is better used for movies and TV shows. The screen should be able to display 100% DCI-P3 colors. The future standard is BT.2020, which is better used for ultra-high-definition video. The screen should be able to display 100% BT.2020 colors in the near future.

4. The best principles of refresh rate: the faster the screen refreshes, the smoother and more realistic the visual effect is. The screen refresh rate is measured by how many times per second the screen changes the image. The current standard is 120Hz.

5. The best principles of BPP - bits per pixel: the more bits used for each pixel - which includes red, green, and blue, the more gray scale of each sub-pixel, the more sum colors can be displayed on each pixel, and the smoother color transitions. The number of colors of each sub-pixel is $2^{\wedge}$(the number of BPP), the number of colors of each pixel is $2^{\wedge}(3 \times$ the number of BPP). The screen should use the original bits - not the processed bits - to display the colors. More bits mean more color perception. BPP is related to color gamut, but they have different goals. The current standard is 10, which means the screen can display over a billion colors.

6. The color depth and the color gamut are the settings that determine how many colors a screen can display. The color accuracy makes it clear how close the screen colors are to the colors of the real world. The color depth and the color gamut coverage are on the stage and the color accuracy is the performer.
7. The best principles of brightness: the brightness of the screen should be as close to the brightness of the real world as possible. The brighter the screen, the better, until it reaches the same level as reality. The brightness of the screen is made by light-emitting areas or LEDs, which are very small. If there is any difference between them, it can make the screen look uneven. To avoid this, the light-emitting areas or LEDs should be as consistent as possible. And the closer to 100% unification, the better. The current standard is 1000 nits to 2000 nits.
8. The best principles of contrast ratio: the greater the contrast ratio of the screen, the better the black display effect.
9. The best principles of display/encapsulation technology: if the display effect was enhanced, it could be mentioned appropriately. For instance, encapsulation technologies that make the screen thinner.

10. The best principles of a viewing angle: the wider the viewing angle, the more consistent experience of different perspectives.
11. OLED panels currently dominate the market. However, the industry is rapidly shifting its focus towards the future potential of MicroLED technology. But there is still a problem with the high power consumption while displaying the white color.

V The logical ppi they claimed is not the effective ppi that our eyes directly perceive. The logical ppi can be misleading.

You may have heard PPI - pixels per inch - a term that measures how sharp a screen is. But do you know that the PPI can be misleading, especially for OLED screens? Logical PPI is confusing and replacing the inherent perception of effective PPI. Let me explain.

PPI was popularized by Steve Jobs when the iPhone 4 debuted with a Retina screen. He claimed that the human eyes could not see individual pixels at a certain distance, and that the iPhone 4 had reached that limit. Back then, the mainstream screen on the market was based on the TFT-derived screen with RGB arrangement, where each pixel had three sub-pixels - red, green and blue - of the same size. The logical PPI of the screen was equal to the amount of effective PPI on the screen.

However, OLED screens use a different arrangement in which each pixel has larger red and blue sub-pixels with smaller green sub-pixels. This means that each pixel takes up more space on the screen, and the screen can fit fewer pixels in total. For example, a P-arrangement OLED screen has about 1/3 fewer pixels than an RGB-arrangement LCD screen of the same size. This reduces the effective ppi of OLED screens, which is the actual sharpness that you perceive. In other words, effective PPI < logical PPI for OLED screens. You can notice this difference when you look at the details and edges of the texts on the screen.

So, if you compare two screens with the same size and resolution, the LCD screen will have higher effective PPI than an OLED screen, and the image will look clearer and smoother. And if you compare two OLED screens with the same resolution, the larger one will have lower effective PPI than the smaller one, and the texts will look more jagged and blurry.

This is why the iPhone X's screen - which used OLED technology - is less detailed than the iPhone 8 Plus's screen, which used LCD technology, even though they have similar resolutions. And this is why the 2K OLED screens on the latest flagship mobile phone may not look as good as the 2K LCD screens on the older ones. Personally, I would prefer the top 2K LCD screen over the 2K OLED screen.

If you want to estimate the effective ppi of your OLED screen, you can multiply the advertised PPI by 2/3. This is a rough approximation that works for P-arrangement Samsung OLED screens, but it may vary for other brands.

V The innovative direction of OLED in the future

'PPI has no need to be improved' is an example of how they escape the responsibility of screen innovation.

Speaking of PPI, it's important to mention the innovations of the screen. I find it hard to imagine that the current direction of screen upgrades is to simply increase the maximum brightness of the screen. I wonder if the brightness of individual pixels, brightness of area, and brightness of the whole screen can be consistent.

The ultimate goal of the screen is to infinitely reproduce the visual effects that are close to the real world, to fake reality. The enhancements that can be expected at present are the expressiveness of the screen colors, physical form, and physical structure. Color expressiveness is associated with the BPP - bits per pixel - of the screen, the color accuracy of each pixel of the screen, and power consumption control. The physical form and physical structure expressiveness are associated with the PPI of the screen, that is, the resolution. As the mainstream market is currently dominated by OLED screens, the life of the pixels is the biggest constraint, and improving the color performance will increase the power consumption of the screen. Therefore, power consumption control is also a basic support requirement to match.

Don't be fooled by mobile phone manufacturers' propaganda that 'beyond an effective PPI of 300PPI - Apple follows the Retina-level of 326PPI or equivalently close to it - there is no need to upgrade the PPI - instead, it increases the power consumption in vain'. These are incompetent words. Firstly, the standard Retina-level is affected by distance and the consumers' eyesight, which will cause big fluctuations. Considering the wide range of eyesight of the user group, there is still a lot of room for PPI improvement. Secondly, we use the screen as a carrier to receive the visual information, not to distinguish the pixel points.

Mobile phone screen resolution from 360p to 1080p to 2K to 4K has verified that the higher the PPI, the closer the visual effect is to reality.

Next, we just need to study whether going beyond 300PPI has a positive impact on the visual effect.

Let's do an experiment. Half a meter away from the screen, respectively, observe a lady's hand and the photos of the lady's hand that show on the mobile phone screens with 2K and 4K resolution. We can feel a huge difference in the visualization of the three scenes, not only between 4K and the lady's hand, but also between 2K and 4K. That is because in the microcosm - we imagine the lady's hand as a screen - the smallest unit of the lady's hand is the skin cells, compare with the smallest unit of the screen pixels, which differ by several magnitude orders. This leads to the macrocosm looking different. That is to say, under the condition of not being affected by the factors of sight and distance, when the PPI is continuously increased to infinitely close to the smallest constituent unit of the object's surface, its visual effect will continue to converge on the real object, but there will always be a certain difference from the real object.

Take another example that is easy to understand. For example, skincare promotes a tighter arrangement between skin cells in the microcosm, thus making the skin in the macrocosm have a smoother and tighter visual effect.

Let's do another experiment. Through the distance of half a meter and 3 meters respectively, observe a lady's hand and the photos of the lady's hand that show on the mobile phone screens with 2K and 4K resolution. At the distance of half a meter, we may just feel the lady's hand with significantly different visual differences. But at the distance of 3 meters, we may have a hard time making sure that the lady's hand photos on a 4K resolution screen is a hand. The photo of a lady's hand on the 2K resolution screen has been difficult to distinguish, but the eyes can still be sure that the lady's hand is the hand. That's because as the distance increased, the amount of visual information that can be captured by our eyes decreased. This may be the excuse that mobile phone manufacturers thought there was no need to upgrade the resolution of the screen. But upgrading the screen resolution reduces the loss of visual information at a distance, thus retaining more recognizable information. The effect of eyesight follows a similar logic, with good eyesight determining the quality of visual information captured.

In the above experiments, whether it were skin cells or pixels, they were the microscopic causes of the macro visual effect. And the visual information we receive focuses on the macroscopic presentation. So the PPI of the microscopic world is just an imperceptible marketing word.

By now, everyone should have understood the significance of the PPI increase - the resolution of the screen. Let's move on to BPP - bits per pixel - which affects the screen's color performance, and each pixel affects the screen's color grade.

According to The Art Of iPhone Review, we understand that the larger the BPP - bits per pixel - the more gray scale of each sub-pixel, the more sum of colors displayed on each pixel, and the smoother color transitions. The number of colors of each sub-pixel is $2^{\wedge}$(the number of bpp), the number of colors of each pixel is $2^{\wedge}(3 \times$ the number of bbp).

That is to say that BPP broadens the boundaries of our perception of color. Similar logic applies to the color gamut, but it needs further planning, and now the mainstream DCI-P3 color gamut still has a lot of room for development, so it will not be mentioned again.

Color accuracy is a frequently mentioned issue. The color accuracy determines the degree of screen color reproduction of reality. The closer the screen's color performance is to the real world, the better its color accuracy. Since the smallest color display unit of a screen is a pixel, microscopic differences can have a noticeable effect in the macroscopic world. And in order to eliminate this effect, it is necessary to ensure a highly uniform color accuracy in each pixel. The color accuracy of all pixels is closer to 100% uniform, the more abruptions of the bad pixels.

BPP and color gamut are the stage, and color accuracy is the performer.

To achieve the above elements of enhancement, more screen power consumption is inevitable, but this is a problem that technology should overcome, rather than an excuse to escape. Improving the development of better substrates, smaller currents' excitation, and finer color management are all possible directions for breakthroughs. Especially the white color display of today's mainstream

OLED, the rumor is that 'OLED is more power-efficient than LCD', and I'm ashamed of the handset makers who advertise it as such. If that's the case, you need to make sure the screen's main display color is black. But it is against human nature. After all, human beings are born to recognize the beautiful world in the light of day. How can they live in the dark? Dark mode is only for emergencies. Similarly, the lifespan of a pixel point is equally crucial. Existing technologies are already lagging behind the needs of the entire era, so how can they not catch up?

In fact, in the final analysis, all the artificial definitions are driven by their respective interests, and in the name of science, they are all manifestations of ignorance about the potential and adaptability of human senses. From frugality to luxury is easy. It is not a result, but a process. There is no most extravagant, only more extravagant, which is human desire.

In short, the ultimate development goal of the digital world is the real world, and the ultimate development goal of the real world is the digital world, but they can only ever be on the way.

V CPU & GPU

The best principles: it determines the entire quality of mobile phone calculation. It is better to compare with the same platform or the previous generation. The most important thing is peak performance & power-efficiency.

Examples of Apple Chips:

Apple's iPhone A series chip has always been the strongest and most dominant in the mobile phone market, because Apple relies on this chip to lead the technology strategy. In the past, we did not care much about how powerful the A series chip was, but we felt that it could make the iPhone run very smoothly and efficiently in any situation. This meant that the A series chip was always stronger than what the peak performance the iPhone needed.

However, that changed when the iPhone 11 series added the feature of night mode. A series chip could not handle the night mode processing fast enough, and it showed that it lacked enough power of calculation. This problem was not solved until the iPhone 14 pro series with the A16 chip.

If the A13 chip of the iPhone 11 series showed the A-series chip cannot efficiently reach the peak performance demand at the hardware & software calculation-level, then from the A16 chip of the iPhone 14 pro series, the iPhone was unable to maintain a daily and efficient use of 48-megapixel in the peak performance scenario of 48-megapixel ProRaw, which also meant that the A-series chip had become a hindrance to the hardware.

There are two critical points here: one is when the hardware and software could not keep up, and one is when the hardware could not keep up. A series chip lost its advantage of being stronger than what the peak performance the iPhone needed, and this was a turning point for Apple's iPhone chip strategy.

However, Apple is still making some confusing decisions, such as using the same A15 chip for both the iPhone 13 Pro and the iPhone 14, and using the same A16 chip for both the iPhone 14 Pro and the iPhone 15. Apple needs to wake up! If Apple doesn't, Apple will lose their technology leadership with their chips, and this will affect their high-end brand strategy. Other things like IOS stability, functionality, and maturity are also facing some challenges. Although these strategic factors have a long-term impact that can last for years or decades, relying on old achievements will eventually lead to a sudden collapse, but rebuilding a strategy is not a quick process.

V Modem-RF Systems

The best principles: It determines how well the mobile phone can connect and communicate with other devices and networks. It depends on many factors, such as the type of cellular technology, the speed and quality of the signal, the ability to use different frequency bands, the ability to reduce noise and interference, the ability to adjust the power and direction of the signal, the maximum download and upload speed, the efficiency of data transmission, and the power consumption of the mobile phone. These factors should be mentioned when they change significantly or when the mobile phone uses a different brand of technology.

V RAM - An important key indicator for a mobile phone used for more than three years - related to the control of the IOS ecosystem

1. The best principles of capacity: the larger the capacity, the larger the background task capacity and the better user experience of third-party applications.

2. The best principles of DDR generation: the higher or newer the generation, the better the performance.

3. The best principles of main frequency: the higher the main frequency, the faster its speed.

4. The best principles of timing order: the lower, the better.

5. The best principles of stability and reliability: the less data loss, the better.

6. The best principles of performance change: as time passes by, the performance decreases less, the better.

7. Apple is losing control over the IOS and iPhone ecosystems. One example is the bad experience of IOS killing the background applications, which shows that Apple did not plan and control the IOS ecosystem well. Another example is the sudden increase in RAM for different iPhone models, which creates a lot of fragmentation and confusion for developers and users. It also makes the iPhone less efficient and reliable. I remember the days when the iPhone had 1G RAM, and it could keep the applications content even after it restarted. But the days are gone.

V Camara system - image sensor, integrated or independent ISP, lense

1. The best principles of area per pixel: the larger the area per pixel, the better the luminous flux.
2. The best principles of light-sensitive capacity per pixel: the stronger the light-sensitive capacity per pixel, the more accurate the color and light of the image.
3. The best principles of total pixels: the more the number of pixels, the more details and resolution the image has.
4. The best principles of pixel layers: the more transistor pixel layers, the better the luminous flux.
5. The best principles of the active area of the image sensor: the active area is usually smaller than the image sensor, and located in the middle of the image sensor. Active area size depends on the aspect ratio of the image sensor and the aspect ratio of the output image of the camera. The active area size can depend on different scenes.
6. The best principles of lenses: these are glass or plastic lenses that focus and shape the light before it reaches the image sensor. The more lenses, the better the optical system can correct for distortion, aberration, and vignetting. Glass lenses are better than plastic

lenses because they have higher clarity and transmittance.

7. The active area size and lens focal length determine angles of view.

8. The best principles of signal-to-noise ratio: the higher the signal-to-noise ratio, the cleaner and sharper the image is.

9. The best principles of focusing: ①Hybrid focus: This is a combination of different focusing methods that can cover a wider range of scenes. The actual performance depends on how well the phone optimizes the focus. ②PDAF phase focusing: This is a fast focusing method that uses the phase difference of light to measure the distance. However, it needs good lighting and contrasting conditions. Advanced PDAF dual-core focus or full pixel dual-core focus are improved versions that are both fast and accurate. ③Laser focusing: fast, but it has a short working range and may not work well in bright or reflective environments. ④Contrast Focusing: Slow but accurate.

10. The best principles of anti-shake: Sensor-shift is the strongest type, as it moves the sensor itself to compensate for the shake. OIS optical stabilization is the second-strongest type, as it moves the lens elements to stabilize the image. EIS electronic

stabilization is the weakest type, as it uses software to crop and adjust the image.

IV Quality Reliability

V Structural strength

The best principles: the more solid the mobile phone, the more resistant it is to damage or deformation. The stability depends on how the inside components of the mobile phone are fixed. The higher the double-sided fixation rate, the more stable and secure the internal structure of the mobile phone is.

V Production-level

The best principles: the less the error between components, the higher the quality and precision of the production process. The production level can be measured by how many defective pieces are found in numerous components. The standard is only allowed one defective piece per 10,000 pieces.

V Quality Control Level

The best principles: this is how well the mobile phone is checked and verified before it is sold. The mobile phone should have as few defects as possible, which means that it works properly and does not have any problems or errors. The quality control level can be measured by how many defective mobile phones are found in numerous mobile phones. The standard is only allowed two defective mobile phones per 20,000 mobile phones.

V Performance of drop resistance

The best principles: the mobile phone should be able to resist damage and keep working after being dropped. The level of drop resistance can be measured by how many times the mobile phone can be dropped from a certain height without being broken. The standard is to keep the mobile phone still working after 20 drops from 2 meters.

Why was the iPhone 12 Pro's frame less drop resistant compared to the iPhone 11 Pro's frame? It involved a mechanical structural issue. You can think of the iPhone 11 Pro's frame as an arch bridge. When the impact occurs, the arch is subjected to a vertical downward force Q, and the frame support connected to the arch will generate a vertical reverse force V and a horizontal thrust H. Due to the existence of the horizontal thrust H, the bending moment of the arch will be much smaller than that of a beam of the same span, and the whole arch bridge will shoulder the pressure. Figuratively speaking, it means that when the iPhone 11 Pro's frame is impacted, the entire arch frame shoulders the pressure, while only the impacting part shoulders the pressure when the iPhone 12 Pro is impacted.

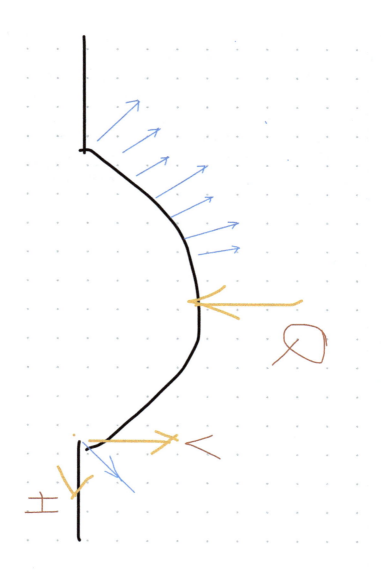

V IP-level

The best principles: the higher the IP-level, the better quality. It is the IP68 Age.

IV Safe

The best principles: the mobile phone should not have any risk of exploding or catching fire due to overheating, overcharging, or physical damage. The potential risks should be within safe and controllable limits.

IV Craft

The best principles: the mobile phone should also use advanced and innovative craft techniques to produce. It deserves respect and appreciation if the craft behind the product is important and meaningful.

III Comprehensive Experience

This is how the mobile phone feels in your grip when you hold it and use it. It depends on how much pressure the mobile phone puts on your palm and fingers. The pressure comes from the weight of the mobile phone, the shape of the mobile phone, and the way you grip the mobile phone.

Here are some factors that affect the pressure:

The contact area between the mobile phone and your palm: The more curved the mobile phone's sides are, the more contact area there is. The more flat the mobile phone's sides are, the less contact area there is. If the mobile phone has the same weight and shape, the less contact area there is, the more pressure, and the less comfort for your palm.

The weight of the mobile phone: The heavier the mobile phone, the more pressure it puts on your palms and fingers. If you just hold the mobile phone without using it, the pressure mainly comes from the weight of the mobile phone. The heavier the mobile phone, the less comfort for your palm.

The interaction with the mobile phone: When you use the mobile phone, you need to move your fingers to touch different sections of the screen. You will grip it harder to stop the mobile phone from dropping or shaking. And you need to push against the edge of the mobile phone to stretch your finger if you need to interact in a far section of the screen, then the smaller the thickness of the mobile phone, the easier interaction at a long-distance. These actions increase the pressure on your palms and fingers. The more you interact with a mobile phone, the less comfort for your palm.

The actual mechanics of the mobile phone in your hand are more complex, and different parts of your hand may feel different pressures.

IV Thin Technology

The demand for a "thin" mobile phone is not a direct one, but rather an indirect expression of a deeper need.

It's well-known that the mobile phone is a highly integrated smart device. Usually, the higher the integration of electronic components, the thinner the mobile phone will be in macro-visual terms. This is a common sense in electronics. So, when we see a thin mobile phone, we associate it with advanced technology and innovation.

But thinness is not only a psychological and visual preference, it is also a practical demand. A thinner mobile phone makes it easier to hold and interact with one-hand.

Therefore, thinness is a way of showing that we want a mobile phone that has advanced technology, an attractive design, and a comfortable user experience. It is a comprehensive expression of our potential needs.

IV Unlock System

Normal human behavioral inertia is continuous and efficient, so try to break down tasks within behavioral inertia and avoid any disconnected behaviors coordinated by the brain. The object of the action can change - for example, from fingerprint recognition to facial recognition on the front of the mobile phone, but the action itself should keep the same - for example, unlocking from the front instead of the rear.

That is why I do not agree with the idea of double-sided interaction on a normal-sized phone. It creates a paradox: if the front and the rear have different functions, then the users have to learn how to use them differently, which complicates things. Including but not limited to photo taking, screen effects, unlocking, and so on. This goes against the human desire for simplicity. But if the front and the rear have the same functions, then no two sides are needed.

When it comes to unlocking a mobile phone, there is no clear winner between fingerprint and facial recognition. They both have their advantages and disadvantages in terms of convenience, speed, and experience.

But in some special situations, like a pandemic, fingerprint recognition might be more useful. However, we cannot predict the future, so it might be wise to integrate both technologies and be ready for any situation.

II Industrial design of software

III UI

Most of them can refer to the industrial design of the entire sights of hardware. Here is the additional content to show the bellowing.

IV Color

The best principles: main colors should match the design style. The color should not be tiring the eyes, and the number of colors should be less than four. If multi-color are used, they should be used in small areas.

IV Space

1. The best principles of comfort: the more comfortable the entire layout, the better the visual effect.
2. The best principles of reasonableness: the more reasonable the entire layout, the better the visual effect.
3. The best principle of spatial utilization: the higher the entire space utilization rate, the better the visual effect.

IV Font & icon - the most basic visual information element - where the eyesight stays longest.

1. The best principles of exquisite: the more exquisite the font, the better the visual effect.

2. The best principles of unity: the more uniform the font, the better the visual effect.
3. The best principles of harmony: the more harmonious the font or multiple fonts, the better the visual effect.
4. The best principles of easily reading: The higher the legibility of the font, the better the visual effect.
5. The best Chinese font is the Hiragino KakuGothic - ヒラギノ角ゴシック体 - designed by the Japanese. The best English fonts are found in the Western world.
6. The basic visual information element determines the final product design.

IV The importance of a font for the OS

Take the same Apple system fonts as an example, the Japanese font Hiragino Kaku Gothic ProN - ヒラギノ角ゴシック体, the Simplified Chinese font Apple Pingfang. Here we do not delve into font specifications such as glyphs, center area, skeleton, etc., but only start from the perceived visual.

Hiragino Kaku Gothic ProN is an artwork-like font that puts esthetics as its first priority, making it pleasing to the eyes; Apple Pingfang puts functions as first priority, it focuses on font specification with a little bit of Apple's unique quest for legibility and esthetics.

A single control variable, take simplified Chinese as reference. At first glance, Hiragino Kaku Gothic ProN looks mainly square-shaped and strict - but with a lively spirit. It has a lot of details that catch your eyes and make you want to enjoy yourself closer. When you look at it, you'll get to know that the designer has thought about esthetics, such as detail that goes a little beyond the junction, such as the barbs that have been abandoned, and such as the use of a horizontal stroke instead of a point. Throughout the font, Hiragino Kaku Gothic ProN adds, deletes, adjusts, and changes some details according to different words. It doesn't simplify the strokes to cater to digital display, but rather pursues the spirit and essence of the font. Under the uniform style where esthetics is the first priority, each word competes with the other. This kind of detail goes far beyond the realm of the bland Apple Pingfang, which sacrifices esthetics for legibility.

In actual scenarios. Apple Pingfang allows me to quickly understand what the word was trying to present, while Hiragino Kaku Gothic ProN is able to draw me in with more desire to explore each word. Freshness is a factor, but probably a more important factor is the eyes discovering something even better at first glance.

That's why Hiragino Kaku Gothic ProN is known as "Japanese Helvetica". This is also the reason why I changed the system's language to Japanese. Art No Borders, I am willing to put up with inconvenience for the sake of this aesthetic.

Because the visual area of a word is small, a slight angle adjustment of a stroke, a small change in the direction of a point, shortened 0.1 mm, etc. will be very intuitively reflected in the font. Font designers are supposed to ensure the beauty of individual words, must ensure the unity of the coordinated beauty when words are gathered on a screen, and then expand the unity of the beauty to thousands of words. It's a giant project.

Of course, I don't like the Hiragino Kaku Gothic ProN as a whole font. Because katakana and kanji are intertwined, it looks fine when kanji dominate katakana, but it's hard to avoid katakana dominating, or even worse. The parallel styles of the two are not similar to each other, they will form a strong abruptness. Therefore, the use of these two styles, tends to create a lack of clarity in terms of priority, which is not as good as the uniform esthetics.

Many people may lack a sense of esthetics, but it is only when things change in a way that causes them to feel nitpicked, lost, or compromised, then they become acutely aware of the difference between beautiful and ugly. Therefore, aesthetic fatigue is not a reason for Apple's San Francisco becoming more ugly than Helvetica.

IV The best principles of comprehensive screen layout: the layout of the content is clear, and different information elements are controlled within four.

III UX

The best principles: The fastest and most pleasurable way to get what users demand.

IV Simulation of physical properties

The best principles: motion should follow the laws of physics, such as inertia, bounce, and non-linear speed changes. This makes it more intuitive and comfortable.

IV Interactive Logic

The best principles: the design should have clear and logical layers, minimize the number of steps, and avoid confusing the user - for example, a foldable phone should have two independent forms that work as separate "mobile phones" and "tablets". The design should also avoid mixing different functions in the same interaction.

IV Interactive area

The best principles: the design should consider the finger size and the habitual areas of the user. The design should make it easy and comfortable for the user to interact with the mobile phone. As the mobile phone gets taller, the interactive core area gets lower.

IV Interactive method

The best principles: the design should use different gestures for different purposes. Click is good for precise actions, slide can be used as a supplement of non-click interactive to the interactive logic layer, and multi-finger interactive can cover large areas. The design should also use eye-catching colors for neutral pages, vibrant interaction, and sound interaction to make them more efficient. Respond to visual interactions with visual feedback, respond to auditory interactions with auditory feedback, respond to tactile interactions with tactile feedback.

IV Feedback

The best principles: any interaction needs feedback to make sure the action was recognized by the mobile phone, but it can be visual, auditory, or tactile. The faster feedback speed within the range, the better.

V Comfortable sight

The best principles: the animation should have a non-linear speed change to make it more comfortable. The animation should change from a shorter and gradually decreasing strength to longer and gradually decreasing strength smoothly. The smoother the curve changes, the more comfortable it feels. This is an advanced review item.

V Stable frame rate

The best principles: the performance of frame rate should be consistent without frames being dropped in every situation to create a better experience.

V Animation detail

The best principles: the richer the details in every frame, the more delicate it looks, but it needs to avoid the visual fatigue caused by excess.

V Transition

The best principles: the smoother the transition, the better the natural experience.

V Animation time

The best principles: animation time should last as long as reality and not too long or too short. The time of gradual increase in strength is shorter than the time of gradual decrease in strength. For example, a touch that lasts too long or too short may feel unnatural and abrupt.

III OS

IV Stability

The best principles: the higher the stability, the more trustworthiness.

IV Performance Optimization

The best principles: the system should run as fast and smoothly as possible in different situations.

IV Applications Management Mechanism

The best principles: the system should have a good mechanism to manage the applications in front and background, so that the user can switch between them easily, work more efficiently, and save battery life.

IV Ads Management

The best principles: there should be no ads that affect the user experience in the system and built-in applications. The ads for third-party applications should not exceed the user's tolerance limit, and try to maintain a consistent visual effect with the content in the application, and should not be presented in a separate from - includes notification, pop-up, full-screen.

IV Battery Life Optimization

The best principles: the higher the level of fineness in every situation, the better the optimization, and the longer the battery life.

IV Control Of Ecosystem

The best principles: the system should have a high-level of control over the App Store ecosystem, so that the applications developed by a third party can match the user experience of the built-in applications.

IV Ecosystem Strength

The best principles: the more exclusive applications, the bigger ecosystem strength. Mention the exclusive applications according to your daily usage habits.

IV Exclusive Features

1. Highlight features that improve the daily usage of most users.
2. Low-frequency features that benefit specific groups of users based on their needs.

IV OS Upgrade Cycle

The best principles: the system should have a long OS upgrade cycle that maintains the same or similar user experience - performance decreased less than 20% than a new mobile phone. Ideally, the system should last for at least five years, which is the normal lifespan of a mobile phone.

IV Bugs

The best principles: the more bugs, the worse the experience. The closer to the bottom layer, the worse.

1. Bugs didn't appear with old features yesterday, and are also not allowed to appear with old features today. People may make mistakes, but shouldn't make mistakes that they wouldn't have made yesterday.
2. Daily usage level bugs should not appear, none is acceptable.
3. Security and performance bugs should not occur. No more than 3 in a month, and try to solve the problem within a month after it is discovered.
4. Low-frequency bugs should be avoided. No more than 1 in a half year, and try to solve the problem in the next big update after it is discovered.

III The consequences of breaking the design concepts left behind by Mr. Jobs

Post-Jobs Era. About the new iOS features - at the level of OS - Apple broke the design concepts of the best visual-efficiency - putting function ahead of design. In the level of built-in applications - the updates were not bad - no big harm to design - mainly to continue the design concepts.

Fortunately, the IOS upgrades have had fewer changes in recent years. So the harm to IOS was less than 23%.

Take the debut of IOS 16 as an example.

1. It was a funny story about the customizable lock
    screen for Apple's top design team in the world. They
    had the top professional design skills - no-one could

catch up and could provide the best design to pleasure anyone - but they lost confidence to believe that the unprofessional consumers can make the best design to make themselves happy. Don't shirk responsibility to customers just because you were lazy or tight-fisted. There were lots of such kinds of things, such as the bottomed floating search bar on Safari in the early IOS 16 beta.

2. The chaos logic between the widgets on the lock screen and the bottom notifications. Apple moved the notifications to the bottom for better wallpaper show, especially for depth wallpaper. Then IOS killed the depth feature of wallpaper for a better widget show. But the notifications have first priority on the lock screen for consumers. So Apple had to correct it - giving the users a complex option to customize the notification styles after later update. There were lots of such kinds of things, such as the overlap features in the early IOS 16 Photos between the double touch to zoom in and select texts.

3. The bigger customizable fonts on the lock screen were as Apple wished. As low as making a bigger Apple Logo on a MacBook. You can be far away from exquisite if you just put something bigger. At the same time, it broke the unity of the fonts on the lock screen.

4. Too much non-unification. Such as, the widgets and icons, the older widgets on the left screen of the home screen and the new widgets, the background applications list arrangement and the pages list arrangement on Safari. Refer to third-party applications, the non-unification more than that.
5. The stability of IOS got worse and worse. The bugs that didn't show before showed. From rare scenarios to daily scenarios.

So, you should get used to the fact that IOS gets worse and worse as new features are added.

III Apple's control of the iOS ecosystem and iPhone ecosystem is getting worse

One bad experience is the iOS killing the background applications, which shows that Apple's control of the iOS ecosystem is getting worse. This is also related to Apple's control of the iPhone, which is also getting crazy.

Remember that Apple's executive said IOS does not need to kill the applications in the background. IOS background management could support this statement. It saved the power to calculate and read data when reloading. But the truth was that IOS 15 got a chance to reload the applications, it showed that IOS background management was dead.

Apple has to make a good plan for the RAM to keep a good experience with applications. Apple needs to plan based on whether the RAM is taken by IOS and the RAM is left to applications.

The problem was that IOS lost control of the RAM left to applications. Because each generation of iPhone had at least 4 big IOS upgrades, the coexistence of 2G RAM, 3G RAM, 4G RAM, 6G RAM led to fragmentation of IOS. Apple had to make a choice - put the newest two generation iPhone first - and sacrificed the older generation's iPhone, so did the developers. I don't believe that the developers will force themselves to perfect the applications by checking the codes line by line for a better user experience. The times have gone.

If Apple can kill bugs to take back control of the ecosystem through IOS upgrades, then it's almost impossible to correct the problem that the RAM led to the loss of control of developers.

The sudden increase in RAM has created a big gap between different generations of the iPhone. At the same time, the RAM increases more and more frequently.

I really miss the old days when the iPhone had 1G RAM. Even if I restarted the iPhone, the previous applications' content was still there.

That's not the end. Apple also lost control in other fields.

In just two years, the bottom of the iPhone 13's notch and the iPhone 14 Pro's dynamic island have been moved down twice. This has increased the adaptation work for iOS developers and has affected the content creators as well.

Maybe the crazy starting point was when the iPhone 12 changed its screen size to 6.1" from the iPhone 11 Pro's 5.8". The 0.3" didn't bring much improvement or difference, but the flatted frame and wider body brought a terrible grip experience. And it left more problems for iOS developers to keep up with the change.

You can see that the perfect iPhone & iOS are being ruined bit by bit.

III IOS 17 widget is an ugly and inefficient industrial design element on the iPhone

Since the introduction of the home screen widget in iOS14, I've been less than impressed.

I won't speculate whether Apple learned from Android or Windows Phone, which has more experience in this field. Windows Phone adopted the Metro UI because its design strategy prioritizes information slightly over visual design. However, iOS's design strategy placed a slightly greater emphasis on visual design than on information. These two parallel design concepts clashed on the same page, disrupting the unified aesthetic. Even with Apple's strong design capabilities to enhance the widget, it's hard to conceal its strong sense of fragmentation.

Home screen widgets can be seen as unattractive, and they are often inefficient and cause high-brain-consumption mode.

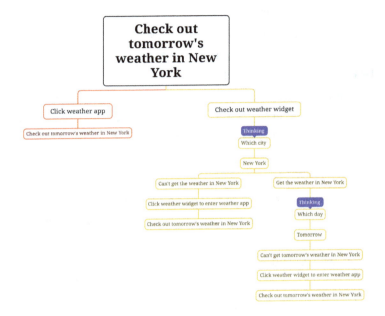

After all, texts are one of the most efficient ways to obtain information. It's a better choice if you view the widget as a means of presenting information, but most of the time the amount of information needed cannot be satisfied by the widget. Once the widget can't meet the information needs, it's necessary to enter the application. The entire home screen can be a trigger of a thought - enter the application or glance at the widget. In this case, it can also lead to a deeper level of thinking - "glance at the widget or enter the application based on information needs". In contrast, the home screen's non-uniform application icons and the low-brain-consumption mode of "one application for one function" undoubtedly consume fewer brain resources. More pessimistically, each application widget corresponds to very specific details, which will increase more brain resources.

A widget at least takes the space of 4 applications, it's low space utilization. As a result, in terms of entire practicality, the iOS home screen widget is inefficient and causes low-brain-consumption mode.

Indeed, widgets have been a part of iOS for quite a long time, but they were initially applied to a dedicated widget hub page that was left on the home screen. This was acceptable for two reasons. First, the widget hub page and the home screen were two separate entities, so there was no sense of fragmentation within the same screen. Second, the uniform widget elements avoided the confusion between widgets and application icons. However, I rarely use the widgets on the widget hub page unless I can manage to 'forget the concept of the application - no need to enter and interact - pure information display area', to avoid entering an extra layer of thought.

What I object to is not the high-brain-consume mode per so, but the non-essential high-brain-consumption mode that reduces efficiency, especially the kind that introduces multiple layers of complex thinking.

For instance, consider the common buttons on an iPhone. When we press the sole power button on the right side, it is easier and more accurate to position when compared to pressing the volume + or - buttons on the left side. So, the power button might be easier to locate, it feels more efficient. However, when we usually press the power button, we can long-press to activate Siri or short-press to turn the screen on or off. This feels less efficient compared to the Ring/Silent switch button.

For mobile phones, the primary logic division is between hardware and software.

The hardware is further divided into six sides of the mobile phone. Each side has upper, middle, and lower zones. Each zone can be divided into upper, middle, and lower segments, and each segment is partitioned to perform specific functions. This is the end of hardware partition.

However, software purely relies on brain memory, not muscle memory. Thus, shallow memory dictates most of our low-brain-consumption mode. The lock screen interface and home screen occupy one layer of partition. The home screen's slide up, slide down, slide left, and slide right actions occupy another layer. The slide down in the left top area to show the notification center and slide down in the right top area to show the control center occupy yet another layer. This is the limit of low-brain-consumption mode.

Overall, the hardware partition is more efficient than the software partition. However, the space of the hardware is limited, which makes it difficult to achieve certain things. For example, the user-friendly design element of 'moving the interactive area to the lower zone' is hard to implement, such as the interactions of sliding down from the top to show the notification center and control center are difficult to move to the lower zone.

III Dynamic Island review - I barely call it a good innovation

Perhaps there is too much love-hate mixed, so many people have a biased perception of Dynamic Island. Although the pill-and-hole was the direct cause of the birth of Dynamic Island, their relationship is not complementary. Simply the pill-and-hole can not get rid of the improvement of Dynamic Island, and Dynamic Island could exist independently without the pill-and-hole. On the contrary, the pill-and-hole greatly restricts the power of the Dynamic Island. Imagine the perfect full-screen iPhone, that kind of amazing visual interaction - from something to nothing, from nothing to something - it has a qualitative improvement than the existence of the pill-and-hole. It's not just the visual impact, but the mental impact.

Dynamic Island, I would like to call it the biggest innovation - since the introduction of human-computer interaction in the mobile phone industry - after 3D touch. Since the introduction of the mobile phone human-computer interaction interface, there has been only gradual innovation and lack of system-level innovation. IOS also can not be immune to this fate. Whether it is the background, control center, notification center, they are all based on the second layer of logic to extend the perfect interaction, while the Dynamic Island is directly based on the first layer of logic to support the interaction of the breakthrough. The innovation closer to the bottom core is often more difficult, and the value of innovation is often incalculable. Not because it is difficult to do, but because it is difficult to think outside the box.

The addition of Dynamic Island is undoubtedly focused on the improvement of the user experience, including the improvement of the visual interaction of Dynamic Island animation and bringing a strong immediate practicality. It also has great potential to unify IOS notification of permission window, App store payment, Apple Pay payment, application notification, volume adjustment and other instant feedback interaction interfaces. If so, it will improve the whole IOS visual interaction unity and coherence further. It can relieve the pressure of the notification center to improve the efficiency of the notification handle.

However, the presence of the pill-and-hole is definitely a blot on Dynamic Island. Visually, the height from the bottom of the pill-and-hole to the top edge bezel exceeded the height of the iPhone 13 Pro's notch, and the height of the iPhone 13 Pro's notch was taller than the Phone 12 Pros'.

The consequences are:

1. Dynamic Island takes at least 4% of the display area forever.
2. Dynamic Island brings at least 10% less display area in the scenario of playing video - that takes up an average of 23% of mobile phone usage times.
3. Apple's call has led many content creators to adapt the Dynamic Island first, sacrificing the user experience of the previous-generation iPhone.
4. The interactive area of Dynamic Island is not conducive to one-hand use and reduces the efficiency of interaction.
5. As I said, "you should get used to the fact that IOS gets worse and worse as new features are added." It includes the Dynamic Island. After a year, Apple only left mixed interactive methods instead of uniform notification interaction.

As the definition of the principle of actual innovation performance: A positive innovation is one that has more strengths than weaknesses, or at least a 7:3 ratio. So we can barely call it a good innovation.

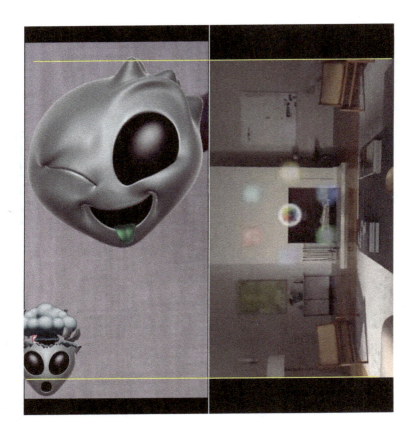

There was a better example - 3D touch - Apple broke the boundaries of hardware and new human-computer interacting solutions. But it became a bad story.

II Innovation

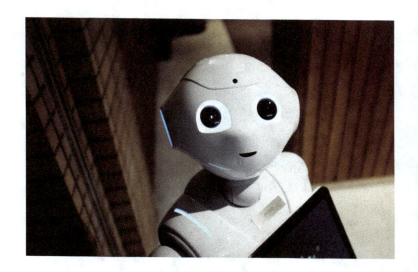

III Perception of Innovation

IV Vertical Innovation

V Disruptive innovation

The best principles: 1, Technology out of the public eyes. 2, Debut in unexpected forms. One cannot exist without the other.

V Incremental innovation

The best principles: technology beyond the reach of rivals or technological advances expected by the public.

IV Horizontal Innovation

It does not offer practical benefits, but it causes subjective novelty. It is also considered a positive innovation because it does not seem like a clear backward.

IV A horizontal innovation has a 1/10 impact of a disruptive innovation at most.

III Practicality of innovation

IV Actual potential needs addressed

The best principles: increase efficiency, expand use scenarios, enhance user experience, and meet at least one of these standards.

IV Actual performance

The best principles: a positive innovation is one that has more strengths than weaknesses, or at least a 7:3 ratio.

III Our expectations of innovation

Nokia's 41 MP CMOS with Pureview technology & Xenon flashlight debuted in 2012, and it was put into the 13.9mm body of the Nokia 808. Next year, Nokia put 41 MP CMOS with Pureview technology into the 10.4mm body of the Nokia Lumia 1020.

The depth of CMOS has been decreased by 3.5mm in 1 year by Nokia. 10 years later today, a 48MP main camera was put into the 8.25mm body by Apple. The depth has been decreased by 2.15mm in 10 years by Apple.

Besides the Night Mode, Sensor-shift, and tetraprism are constrained by the times. I think the development of the technology for the camera is slower than I expected. I also reserve my disagreement on the direction of multiple camera development.

Most importantly, compare the photos taken by the Nokia Lumia 1020 and iPhone 15 Pro. Will you feel a great improvement?

No mention that faster and faster technology is in our expectations. At least, the speed of progress is supposed to keep the same, rather than slower. So do the battery, screen, speaker, technology, UX, and so on.

That's why we feel that innovation has developed slower than our expectations.

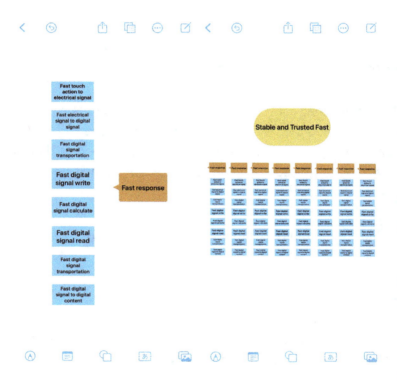

I Chapter 2 Main usage scenarios

II Signal and call

III Signal Quality

The best principles of signal evaluation scenarios: the main test scenarios are the subway and outdoors. The signal performance is better when the comprehensive performance is better.

The signal quality standard within the OS of each mobile phone brand is different, and there is no logical correlation between the signal strength icon and better signal. This is for reference only.

III Call Quality

The best principles: the call quality is better when the call is clearer, more stable, and the human voice is more prominent.

II Internet Surfing

III Cellular & Wi-Fi

IV Connect Speed

The best principles: for the same mobile phone, the connection speed is better when it properly takes less time to connect to cellular or Wi-Fi and start working.

IV Data Throughput (Upload & Download)

The best principles: for the same mobile phone, the bigger throughput of the upload and download of large data, small data, and multiple types of data, the better. The throughput of small data is more important than multiple types of data, and multiple types of data are more important than big data.

IV Stability Of Data Transfer

The best principles: data transfer stability is better when the speed of data transfer is more consistent within each minimum time unit.

IVIntegrity of Data Transfer

The best principles: data transfer integrity is better when less data is lost during data transfer.

III The higher the integration of the system wallet that replaces the physical items, the better the experience

1. Wallet
2. Access card & traffic card
3. Third-party car key & hotel key

III The higher the integration of the Intelligent Product Control Center, the better the experience

1. System integration experience
2. Coverage of intelligent product

III The higher the integration of the AI, the better the experience

II Take photos and shoot videos

III Popular users

IV Experience smoothness

The best principles: the entire process of taking photos from opening the application to getting a picture is smoother, the better user experience.

IV Real Information Collection

The best principles: use real scenes as reference objects, not the photos taken by other mobile phones.

IV Entire Quality

The best principles: minimize the quality difference between the center and edge of the picture.

IV Color and light process / photo resolution / noise control

The best principles: the better control, the better the photo quality.

IV Style orientation / portrait style, landscape, night scenarios, and other special scenarios

The best principles: the better control, the better the photo style.

IV Produce image

The best principles: show the specifications of photo taking - the focal length and the approximate distance of the shot, and the resolution and frame rate for videos - for more credible and accurate reference.

III Professional users

Professional modes and tools

The best principles: The higher the freedom, the higher the ceiling, and the more professional.

IIProductivity

III Coverage of mainstream group's demands: such as mail, web browsing, schedule management, etc.

The best principles: the better the comprehensive quality of the built-in or third-party applications, the better.

III Ecosystem coverage of special group's needs: such as stock, security, digital wallets, network management, music creation, project management, 3D creation, content creation, etc.

1. The more complete the coverage of third-party applications, the better.
2. The higher the comprehensive quality of a third-party application, the better.

II Battery life

The best principles: Test both connection scenarios of home Wi-Fi and outdoor cellular. Since it is impossible to simulate the complex usage scenario of consumers, provide the results of each specific scenario for consumers to evaluate themselves based on their use habits.

Do not review the mobile phone that booted as a new mobile phone or had an OS update within 3 days. Also, do not review right after charging, but wait until at least 2% battery is used.

III Light and single scenario, 5-minute break for every 30 minutes of measurement

1. Social
2. Browser
3. IM
4. Tool
5. Photo/Video

III Heavy and single scenario, 10-minute break for every 1 hour of measurement

1. Game

III Continuous light and single scenarios

1. Write or paint
2. Read or watch movies

III Continuous addictive and single scenario

1. Watch short videos

II Charge

III Wired and Wireless Charging

The best principles: wireless is more free than wired and closer to the future.

IV Charging efficiency

The best principles: the quicker the speed of the charging, the better.

IV Noise Control

The best principles: commonly used in wireless charging, the more noise, the worse the experience.

IV Temperature control and battery life

The best principles: high temperature during charging affects battery life. The better the temperature control, the better the charging experience.

I Chapter 3 Extensions of Product

II Pricing

The best principles: product pricing reflects its entire strength.

II Contribution of Industry

The use or investing in the industry's best technology, product, or craft, which pushes the industry forward.

II Social Responsibility

1. Respect and protect the users' privacy from third-party and first-party parties.
2. Avoid using excessive and false marketing words.
3. Outshine competitors, not undercut them.
4. Wisely use resources as a way of respecting society.
5. Build a positive and corporate culture, and transmit the right values.
6. Elements for determining plagiarism.

①The copycat is usually much weaker than the original in entire strength or global recognition, but sometimes the leader of the industry may copy the runner-up with global recognition to maintain the lead - using a sailing game theory strategy.

②The copycat can only imitate the superficial elements, not the underline reasons. It is hard to grasp the design style/language or even the higher level of the design concept, and the best imitation can only reach 80% of the original. For example, the grip experience of the mobile phone depends on the entire force of the contact area between the mobile phone and the palm, not only on the 'width and thickness of the mobile phone' and other methods that are used to achieve this goal.

③The copycat lacks continuity and plan, and when they feel threat, it abandons its parallel element - even if it is the best globally recognized one - then follows the original. It only shows its ridiculous talent when it gets rid of the threat and becomes arrogance. For example, switch from a hole-punch screen to a notch screen, or from a rounded frame to a flatted frame for a worse grip experience.

④The copycat tends to repeat its behavior, and those who have plagiarized before are likely to do it again.

⑤Due to policies of commercial confidentiality, copy usually starts after the product is released, so the copycat products usually come out later than the original. However, it is possible that copying started when information was obtained from the supply chains or rumors. Even so, because of the development time, the copycat products will not be released much earlier than the original and will not be a good cover for plagiarism.

⑥To hide the fact of plagiarism, the copycat - without the ability to make vertical breakthroughs - will usually do horizontal expansions to mislead consumers with bias.

⑦The copycat usually lacks taste and prefers technical over humanistic and artistic.

II Emotions and Feelings

Personal. For example, the last relics of a grandfather.

/ Chapter 4 Free area

II Popular / unexpected / outstanding advantages or backwardness that individuals care about.

1. DAC adapter cable
2. Bad signal
3. Unlock system with extremely low fingerprints

/ Chapter 5 Review level

II Entry-level

You know the general framework of the review, but not the importance of each level.

II Pro-level

You are skilled in the review framework and the importance of each level.

II Expert-level

You can judge the human nature and trends of some key areas based on an advanced level.

II Master-level

You can envision the next generation mobile device based at an advanced level.

I Chapter 6 Some more things

II Foldable phone and foldable device today and tomorrow. Apple's foldable iPhone & foldable Macbook are on the way

Do you get why Android manufacturers entered a foldable phone product line? Because the high-end Android mobile phone's price is unable to get market recognition. But the innovation of foldable phones is a good reason to convince consumers.

Even though the foldable phone is not the next generation mobile phone, it is still the most important part of the future. It will take about 10% of the mobile phone market. Look at the market for foldable phones. Android foldable phones generally lack competition.

It seems that after such a long time, the foldable phone manufacturers - represented by Samsung - still haven't figured out the definition of a foldable phone, and the vague marketing has led to a mediocre market response.

Steve Jobs defined the iPhone as the iPod & cell phone & internet device when he was competing with traditional cell phones, because the three devices were well known to consumers, and made them clear about their irreplaceable functions & needs & use scenarios. But it doesn't apply to the non-revolutionary evolution of the new foldable phone, which is an integrated product that is both familiar and unfamiliar to consumers, so consumers need clear answers to eliminate uncertainty about this product.

Uncertainty may lead consumers to misunderstand the product, with advantages being ignored and disadvantages being magnified. Promoting the futuristic style and high-tech of foldable phones is emotional marketing, which only works on the premise of a correct definition of the product.

First, the market for foldable phones is competing with the market of smartphones, it must face the users' habits. The form of smartphone does not have much meaning to discuss. The key point is the method of tablet. The obvious difference is the screen's size. The tablet gets better entertainment functions and the productive functions of a light office as the size of screen gets larger.

The factor of value needs to be introduced here. Will the investment of spending twice the price be rewarded accordingly?

At the start point, most people will be more willing to believe that productivity is a valuable return. In reality, the rapid development of the ecosystem over time has made the entertainment of the smartphone become mature. In front of the users' habits, the increased size of the screen may not bring better entertainment. On the contrary, due to limitations of the screen, the productivity of smartphones has always been weak, the increased size of the screen will certainly bring a better experience of a light office.

The market for light office is destined to be smaller than a smartphone and the foldable phone.

I don't like to limit my potential users by their spending power. I prefer to use clear needs to attract many potential users. After all, a very significant percentage of users are willing to sacrifice budgets in other fields for a product that excites them.

In front of professional and productive tools - PCs and laptops - foldable phones still lack competition. Therefore, it must be combined with more special use scenarios. The use scenarios of light office can be excluded from the home and office, which will exist outside the two scenarios, such as a commute.

In summary, we can define that the foldable phone is a 'smartphone & light device for a mobile office'.

My personal needs are for foldable phones that act as 75% smartphone and 25% tablet. So look at the foldable PC. Do you prefer an 'all-in-one PC that folds into a laptop' or a 'laptop that folds into a tablet'?

Time to get back to Apple.

Finally, the foldable MacBook Pro is going to be real as I predicted 1 year ago. The only problem will be the accurate size of the screen. My predicted - height 15.5", width 11.6", folded diagonally length 14", diagonally length 19.4" - due to the diagonal length 19.4" being so close to 20" in the rumors, there is almost no difference.

I premised if the unfolded screen size is 20":

1, if you want the folded screen to be exactly 14", then the folded screen ratio should be 3:2. The unfolded screen ratio should be 4:3. They're two classic productivity ratios.

4:3 applied on the iPad series, 3:2 applied on the Microsoft Surface.

2, if you want the folded screen ratio that is commonly used: 16:9 or 16:10, that folded screen size will be bigger than 14".

In view of:

1, The MacBook is folded for mobility. If the folded screen size is bigger than 14", it loses mobility and the meaning of foldable. The boundaries of the dual-form scenario of the bigger foldable MacBook will be clearer than a foldable phone.

2, The ratio of the Macbook Pro's 14" screen lost control - between 3:2 and 16:10 - and closer to 3:2. If you set free the bottom bezel height of the MacBook Pro, the ratio of the screen will be closer to 3:2.

3, If the height of the touch screen gets higher, it won't make the interactive gets harder, and can obviously improve productivity of contents.

4, Commercial considerations. Both screen ratios are acceptable to users of the mainstream.

5, The future of the foldable MacBook Pro will be created as a brand-new category with a separate OS. Re-planning a new proportion of the specification is not only conducive to brand planning, but also not too difficult for developers.

I think commercial 1 is the biggest possible.

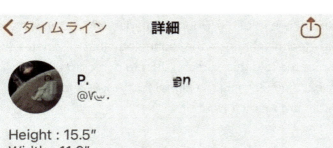

P.　　　　　　　∋n
@Vω.

Height : 15.5″
Width : 11.6″
Diagonally : 19.4″
Fold Diagonally : 14″

↩　　　⇄　　　♡　　　⬆　　　⚙

R2/11/10 at 12:57 via Tweetbot for iOS

↩ 0　　⇄ 0　　❝ 1　　♡ 0

Whether it is a foldable iPhone or foldable MacBook, there is a key technical node - the technology that eliminates the crease of the foldable screen. Just to overcome this technical difficulty, it is the signal that Apple's foldable products are ready for debut.

II Why did Nokia Lumia and Windows Phone fail?

The decline of Nokia was closely linked to the failure of Windows Phone (WP), the operating system Nokia used.

To understand why Nokia failed, we need to look at the reasons why WP did not succeed.

The following picture shows the logic of WP's failure. The gray area represents the final decision to abandon WP, which was influenced by the comprehensive interests of Microsoft shareholders. The light green area represents the direct factors that affected WP's performance, such as the license fee, the Office 365 entrance, and the commission of the developer. The light blue area represents the deep interests of the participants within the WP ecosystem, such as the smartphone manufacturers, the investors, the developers, and the consumers. The red area represents the external competitors of WP, Android and iOS.

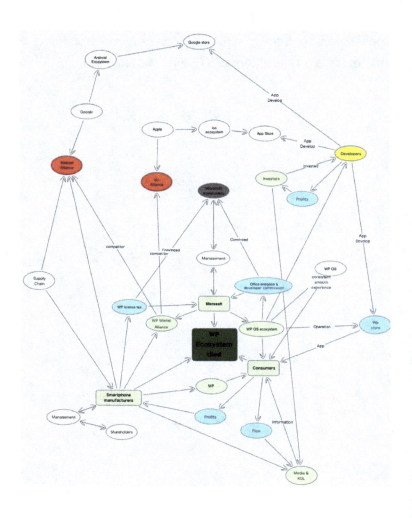

WP's failure can be attributed to four main aspects: the decision of Microsoft's ultimate boss, the strategic planning of Microsoft's ecosystem, the development process of the WP ecosystem, and the market recognition of WP.

1. Microsoft's ultimate boss decided to give up WP because it did not meet their expectations of profit and market share. They realized that they could make more money from Office on iOS and Android, and did not need to rely on WP as their main entry.
2. Microsoft's ecosystem strategy was flawed in several ways. They tried to replicate the model of the Wintel alliance in the mobile phone industry, but failed to compete with iOS and Android. They charged a license fee for WP, which made it less attractive than Android, which was free and widely accepted. They changed the core of the WP several times, which made it incompatible with the previous WP and wasted the resources of the App store. They also limited the differentiation of WP phones, which reduced their market capacity and profit margin.
3. The WP ecosystem development process was hindered by a vicious cycle of interest damage among the participants. The smartphone manufacturers were discouraged by the low sales and profits. The investors didn't like to invest in WP applications due to the small user group. The developers felt unhappy with the frequent changes and low commission of the WP

platform. The consumers felt dissatisfied with the poor quality and variety of the WP applications. The media and KOLs were negative about WP's prospects and reputation.

4. The WP's market recognition was low due to its poor performance in all aspects. It failed to attract enough users, developers, investors, and the media attention. It was overshadowed by Android and iOS, which had more advantages in terms of features, designs, and innovations.

Can HMD Global rewrite Nokia's glory?

I hardly think so. Nokia's mobile phone was eliminated because its ideas could not keep up with the progress of the times. How can HMD Global, which retained the ideas of yesterday's Nokia, lead the way in front of more advanced times?

II Hands-on the best size of Apple iPhone 12, 13, 14, 15 series

After holding them, I felt that iPhone 12 and 13 mini are much better than iPhone 15, 15 Pro and better than iPhone 12, 13, 14 and better than iPhone 12 Pro, 13 Pro, 14 Pro.

It reminds me that Steve Jobs used to say that the golden size of the mobile phone is 3.5 inches, which makes sense in certain circumstances.

The original iPhone had a body of 115mm × 61mm × 11.6mm, the iPhone 4 had a body of 115.2mm × 58.6mm × 9.3mm, and the iPhone 5 had a body of 123.8mm × 58.6mm × 7.6mm. It showed that Steve Jobs followed the idea that the 3.5" screen is the best size of the mobile phone', and he cared about the grip experience and the user experience of one-hand. To be more precise, the width of the iPhone 4 series is 58.6 mm - at that time - the width of the golden size was 58.6mm in the extreme square as technology allowed. That's why the iPhone 3GS width was 62.1mm, but the iPhone 4 - which has evolved to an extreme square - got the smaller width.

So he tried to make the mobile phone as thin and narrow as possible with the technology he had - to make the iPhone 4 easier to hold. And as time went on, he sacrificed some one-hand user experience, but still made the mobile phone thinner and kept the same width - to improve the grip experience of the iPhone 5.

Let's talk about 3.5", which is the expression of his philosophy.

He chose 3.5" by balancing the size of the hand of potential users around the world, from different countries and ages. It was a concept of love, to make the product fit the users' hand comfortably. That's what a product should be. But now the screen size keeps increasing, and it makes more users suffer from its poor grip experience. At the same time, the 3.5" screen kept the finger and could cover 90% of the screen.

Overall, the width of 58.6mm or bigger is not very suitable for a mobile phone of extreme square. If you have to adhere to the form of square, you can properly increase the hold area to balance the pressure. For example, add rounded or chamfered corners at the junction for moderate transition.

Details can not prove a product is good or bad, but can reflect the degree of implementation of design thinking in the whole product.

This shows that Apple's design ability is regressing.

We can also see this kind of regression in many other places, such as the notch, the raised camera bump, and the inconsistent IOS 15 UI design elements, all showing that functions have trumped designs in Apple's evaluation system, even if it's just a small part.

Thanks to Apple, they finally added chamfered corners on the iPhone 15 series after 3 generations.

Today, we can improve the golden width size to 55.6mm. Due to the thinner mobile phone, we can adjust the golden width size to 59mm.

II Front-rear interactive logic like Samsung Galaxy Flip is against human nature

In my perspective, any design that introduces front-rear interactive logic into a normal-sized smartphone is currently against human intuition.

Whether it's yesterday, today, or tomorrow. This includes sub-screens and wraparound screens. These are likely all peculiarities that designers were forced to innovate by their boss. However, making such a counterintuitive design as a selling point is unacceptable!

Who would be willing to pay double or even more than double of the price if the experience on the rear and the front are identical?

That's why the wraparound screen is destined to only attract the attention of investors. If the experience is different on the front and the rear, and one becomes a supplement to the other for specific scenarios, will that enhance efficiency and user experience? Unfortunately, it won't.

When a mobile phone has two screens, it introduces an additional layer of thought on top of the normal use of the mobile phone. Start with a basic judgment of using the front side or the rear side based on fundamental use scenarios. This layer of thought may be very brief, but it exists in all the scenarios where you use the mobile phone, such as text on the front side. However, what's worse is that if this use scenario is subdivided further, it introduces another layer of deeper thought. For instance, you can take a picture on both front and rear sides, but the front camera performs better for selfies and the rear cameras perform better for landscapes. For example, to more conveniently view text messages, should the mobile phone be placed on the front side or the rear side?

Simultaneously, there is a fundamental question about the existence of the secondary screen: can't the functions of the secondary screen be accomplished on the front side? Can't the R&D cost of the secondary screen be used to develop a higher quality front camera?

Since it doesn't function optimally, can you pretend the rear screen doesn't exist? I suppose no one can disregard something that exists with such a strong existence.

The same point in the first paragraph applies to foldable phones. Both forms have a complete and independent form, and both folded and unfolded forms are a separate 'mobile phone'. Once a scenario can only be accomplished in a certain form, it creates an interactive logic of 'front-rear'. The Samsung Galaxy Flip is one such awkward product.

II Android made a bad impression on me. Their skill at propaganda is ahead of 3 gens than user experience.

I tried an Android phone again after 6 years. It was the OPPO Find X3.

I went to a store to get a hand-on. The top and bottom bezels were not satisfactory, and the curved screen on the sides made them more abruption. The 3D curve of the curved screen made the OPPO Find X3 look light and thin. But the areas of the sides that contacted the palm were too small. It was not comfortable to grip.

The 'future streamline design' was a selling point. It would look better if the design was vertical - even though it would make the bump thicker- but it would be more harmony. Some things are not beautiful to be born with - we should try to make them less attractive. Using an asymmetric curve with a strong presence made it twice as bad.

Many tech media and key opinion leaders praised OPPO's OS. They said it was excellent and stable. So I spent half an hour checking it out based on my usual usage.

For the UX, there was a problem with the curved screen. The texts shown in the small bar under the search bar on the Settings page were fuzzy, the font was thinner than the main font. But the texts on the image were not affected. The main font was in the main part of the screen, and the layout of applications rarely touched the curved screen. So this problem was very rare, but it should not happen at all.

For the photo taking, the mobile phone's main camera did well at 1x focal length and within 30cm, it kept more details of the real scene than the iPhone 11 Pro. It showed the benefits of photo capture and display with billion-color. But when I changed the distance to about 5 meters, the photo got worse. The algorithm made the details of the real scene less than the iPhone 11 Pro. The photo experience was not well-optimized. I could see that they put more effort into ordinary scenes.

I did not compare the photos taken by the two mobile phones, but used the real scene as reference.

Comparing the two phones that are shot by two mobile phones is not scientific. There is no standard reference. We should not forget the 'control group' in experiments.

Another confusing point was the texts in the photos. I used the mobile phone's photo editor to add text to a photo, while I double-clicked to zoom in the photo as big as possible, the texts were jagged on OPPO Find X3. But the same actions on the iPhone 11 Pro got smooth. They only became blurred and jagged when I zoomed in to the max. The processing of the texts in the photo on OPPO Find X3 was more like rendering a font rather than a picture.

I only spent half an hour with the OPPO Find X3 - I did not try too much - I only used my daily scenarios. But there were so many problems in these high-frequency scenarios. It showed that this was an untested and immature OS.

Why did OPPO's mobile phones sell better in stores? It mainly depended on the real-time of the information. The shorter the time between getting the information and buying the phone, the more important the information is.

This was my experience in May 2021. It may not reflect the current view.

This proved that Android phones need to be tested in person. After all, Android manufacturers' skill of propaganda ahead 3 gens than user experience.

I was also not happy with the previous review of Android phones. It was not responsible. Here were some problems I found:

- Official images may be optimized or zoomed out, it makes them look better. But it is hard to see the real effect at the smaller size. For example, a fine font may look worse after zooming out. So, we need to use the actual size as a standard reference.
- Some mobile phone makers may use Photoshop to edit their official images. They may do this to increase sales. For example, someone used Photoshop to make the bezels of a mobile phone thinner than it really was.
- I have not seen a picture that showed the true effect of a curved screen. A 3D surface can lose its impact in a

2D picture. Curves can create a sense of order from disorder. But order can also be lost or weakened when mixed with disorder. This can happen with asymmetric curves. Even a small curve can make a big difference.

- The texture and feel of the material are hard to show in a picture. You need to grip the mobile phone in your hand. Then you can feel the touch of the material and the details of its workmanship.

The Android system may not have the exquisite UI. But it can be very practical if there are no bugs. However, in reality, Android bugs won't be disappeared by public relations or by bribing the media + KOLs into silence or by covering this article.

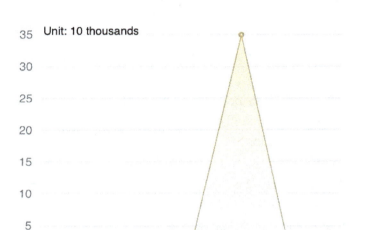

Don't just work hard on the surface, care more about the inside that no one can see.

Last, I don't feel Android phones have too much change.

// We don't want a notch, back fingerprint, or wider bezel.

HOW TO SOLVE THE PROBLEM OF "FULL SCREEN"

"High screen-to-body ratio" is not "full screen", it's just a marketing concept. Misled the development direction of the mobile phone.

It's obvious that we do have potential expectations for "full screen", but "high screen-to-body ratio" is just one point that we're looking forward to. Rise to the entire front also involves the screen-to-body ratio (visual impact), visual coordination of the front, integrity as a screen (visual esthetics), and unlock plan.

The screen-to-body ratio refers to the ratio of the area of the screen to the area of the front panel. Some mobile phone review organizations which are full of pursuit and responsibility introduced a professional word of "average width of bezels" - based on the width of four bezels around the screen - to pull the aesthetic back into the consumers' sight.

The unlock plan is relatively simple. Because of the simple form, it's nothing more than the front unlock system, the back unlock system, the side unlock system, and the hidden unlock system. If the front unlock system gets 100 points. Then, the anti-human back unlock system gets 0 points, the hidden unlock system gets 60 points, and the side unlock system gets 80 points.

It's the "full screen" that we look forward to. If you understand, then you will know, we do not want a notch, back fingerprint, or wider bezel.

So, Apple, you should give up the notch in the MacBook line like the iPhone.

II Will Vision Pro persist until success as Apple Watch?

Why has Apple Watch persisted until success?

First, Apple's impact. Second, the positioning of accessories, so that consumers don't have high expectations for its innovation. Third, the price. Put aside all the marketing elements, it remains a beautiful watch in line with its price.

As my theory, Dimen popularity index = innovation object popularity index + brand coefficient × innovation coefficient × price range coefficient × (annual disposable income per capita / annual disposable income per capita constant) × (consumption habit coefficient / consumption habit constant) / (product pricing / price of innovation object)

Products in the $700-$7000 range:

High-end & well-known brands can maintain their status as mass consumer goods by not exceeding the peak point of (product pricing / price of the innovation object) = 1.

Apple Vision Pro's price is $3499. The minor market has become a market for minorities, and brings about a 10 times market size decrease. At the same time, consumers get higher expectations for its innovation.

The positioning of the next-generation spatial computing devices requires them to have the features completely beyond the iPhone. But the mobility of Vision Pro makes it hard to take the place of the mobile phone. Worse is that

Vision Pro damages the consumer's public and natural image. Precisely speaking, the Vision Pro's competitors are the PC & MacBook.

The third point, once consumers lose interest in the marketing element, what value does the Vision Pro still have, and can this remaining value match its high price? A 3D screen? But it seems that Apple is only getting ready to put 2D content - instead of 3D content - onto this 3D screen.

As I know. Only the second point put Apple in trouble during the Lisa era. Lukewarm VR is just a reflection of reality.

Will Vision Pro persist until success like Apple Watch? I don't think so. At least, the market size is much smaller.

By Shakenal D. G. Dimension

Mar 3, 2024